THE SAGA OF LIFE

"In recent times there has been a proliferation of nursery schools, teen-age centers and homes for senior citizens, all of which isolate people at one stage of the journey from people of all others. The Church remains one societal structure that still seeks to reach out inclusively to the whole human family. Why not, then, attempt to describe the topography of the whole human saga—from womb to tomb—including what unique individuals have in common and some of the challenges they can expect, so that what might otherwise surprise them or seem abnormal in isolation can be anticipated and prepared for in advance?"

—John Claypool

About the author:

JOHN CLAYPOOL has retired recently as Rector of St. Luke's Episcopal Church in Birmingham, Alabama, and is currently serving part-time as Theologian-in-Resident at Trinity Episcopal Church in New Orleans, Louisiana and as Visiting Professor of Homiletics at the McAfee School of Theology in Atlanta, Georgia. He holds the B.A. from Baylor University and B.D., Th.D. from Southern Baptist Theological Seminary in Louisville, Kentucky, and a D.Div. from Georgetown College, Georgetown, Kentucky, in 1971; a D.Laws from Baylor University, Waco, Texas, 1974; D.Div. University of the South, Sewanee, Tennessee, in 1988, and a D.Humane Letters from the Episcopal Theological Seminary of the Southwest, Austin, Texas, in 1998.

THE SAGA OF LIFE

Living Gracefully through
All of the Stages

JOHN R. CLAYPOOL

Insight Press
New Orleans, Louisiana

Published by Insight Press, Inc., P. O. Box 8369, New Orleans,
Louisiana 70182

Cover art by Caroline Humphreys

Scripture quotations are from the Revised Standard Version of
the Bible, by the Division of Christian Education of the National
Council of Churches of Christ in the United States of America,
and are used by permission.

Library of Congress Cataloging-in-Publication Data

Claypool, John .
  The saga of life: living gracefully through all of the stages /
John R. Claypool. – Rev. ed.
        p. cm.
Rev. ed. of: Stages. c1977.
    ISBN 0-914520-43-1 (pbk.)
 1. Christian life–Baptist authors. 2. Life cycle, Human–
Religious aspects–Christianity–Sermons. 3. David, King of
Israel–Sermons. 4. Sermons, American–20th century. 5.
Baptists–Sermons.
I.Claypool, John. Stages. II. Title
 BV4597.555 .C58 2002
 248.4–dc21

2002152080

Dedication

To my dearest wife,
Ann,
who has been my true soulmate
in loving devotion,
tender kindness,
and life-giving wisdom

CONTENTS

PREFACE

It has been over a quarter of a century since the
material in this volume was initially shaped and
articulated. Much has happened in the intervening
years that has genuinely altered the context of
contemporary experience. Yet, beneath all the massive
changes that the information explosion and electronic
revolution have wrought in each of our lives, the basic
landscape of the human saga remains unaltered. We
are still born into this world as tiny infants who move
successively through the stages of childhood,
adolescence, adulthood and, finally, agedness. For that
reason, insights and observations which proved true
and helpful in 1975 continue to be of relevant value in
the dawn of the twenty-first century, prompting the
republishing of this volume.

My gratitude to the good people of Insight Press
continues to grow for their willingness to give new
and continuing life to manuscripts of mine that were

out of print. In particular, Fisher and Caroline Humphreys have played crucial and indispensable roles in what is now our fourth adventure in the process of republication. It was with Fisher's initial encouragement that we began these works of collaboration, and Caroline has masterfully prepared the final typing of these manuscripts as well as having tastefully designed the cover of each. Also, I owe a limitless amount of thankfulness to my beloved partner in life and very best friend, my wife, Ann. Again and again, she has believed in me and in the value of my work. In addition to her unfailing love and support, she had carefully edited, updated and immeasurably improved the initial drafts of this project.

There are feelings of both relief and anxiety when an author releases one of his or her literary creations to the scrutiny and interactions of the larger human family. This revised edition is sent forth in the same hope that accompanied its original mission—that it will bless those whose lives are touched by it.

John R. Claypool
New Orleans, Louisiana
November 20, 2002

INTRODUCTION

THE SAGA OF LIFE

In 1971, I recall saying to my colleagues in religious education that I wished we could pool our insight and outline a spiritual road map for the human saga from womb to tomb. I was fully aware that each individual has his or her own unique experiences along the way, but that at the same time there is much commonality in this journey we are taking. The stages of our lives all follow the same sequential pattern—infancy, childhood, adolescence, youth adulthood, middle adulthood and senior adulthood—and there are many predictable crises and growth challenges that all human beings face despite their individual unique-nesses.

I felt it would be of great value to individuals and to the Church in its program formation to have the benefit of such an overview because, contrary to the familiar adage, what we humans do not know most assuredly can hurt us! I have seen many individuals caught totally unprepared for certain situations in life that seemingly "slipped up on them," particularly in the largest single segment of life—adulthood. Dr. C. J. Jung used to emphasize that the afternoon and evening of life were very different from the morning; the values and strategies that apply to the one do not necessarily work for the others. "Yet where," he asked, "are the universities to prepare us for the last two-thirds of our living?" He accurately pointed out that almost all the emphasis of our educational institutions is focused on getting people ready for the morning period of life—enabling them to gain competence, select a vocation, choose a mate, and so forth.

There really is a gap in terms of serious training for the latter stages of adulthood, and I proposed that the Church was uniquely situated to do something about this vacuum. After all, we are one of the few institutions left in our society that has some kind of contact with all ages of human beings. Too often we are divided not only along racial, social and ideological lines, but also along generational lines. In recent times there has been a proliferation of nursery schools, teenage centers and homes for senior citizens, all of which isolate people at one stage of the journey from people at all others. The Church remains one societal structure that still seeks to reach out inclusively to the whole human family. Why do we not, then, I proposed, attempt to describe the topography of the whole human saga—from womb to tomb—including what unique individuals have in common and some of the challenges they can expect, so that what might otherwise surprise them or seem abnormal in isolation can be anticipated and prepared for in advance?

The idea was greeted with warm enthusiasm, but as so often happens in the daily routine of a big, busy church, nothing was done about it. It was not until four years later, at a winter planning retreat, that the idea resurfaced and this time "became flesh and dwelt among us." We decided then to project a month-long church-wide emphasis on "The Saga of Life" in September, when everyone reconvened after the summer. My contributions were to be sermons on the four basic stages of life, one each Sunday morning. In the evenings we would have dialogue with selected specialists in each of these areas, followed by small group workshops led by teachers in the various departments of our church school, at Broadway Baptist Church in Fort Worth, Texas.

The material that makes up this book is the product of that month of emphasis on "The Saga of Life." It has been tested and enriched by interaction with several other church groups—folk from St. John the Divine Episcopal Church of Houston at Laity Lodge in May, 1976; folk from Second Baptist Church of Lubbock in February 1977; participants at the Christian Life Commission Seminar on "Priorities" in March 1977; and folk at the Murfreesboro Baptist Church in North Carolina. The essence of the content was shaped for and by the congregation in Fort Worth in the fall of 1975.

My aim in these sermons was to blend the light of biblical wisdom with the best information from the behavioral sciences. As a point of focus, I chose the Old Testament figure David, since more material is contained in Holy Scripture about the different phases of his life than of any other individual, with Moses and Joseph running a distant second and third. I thought for a time about using the life experiences of Jesus as the biblical basis, but the scantiness of insight into His childhood and adolescence and the fact that He did not live into "senior adulthood" led me to feel that the legendary King of Israel would be a better resource for this project, though by no means as supreme an example of full humanity. Those readers who are versed in the various disciplines of the behavioral sciences will quickly recognize what I have and have not read among the voluminous possibilities there.

It is just as important to know in advance what these chapters are not as well as what they are, for I have found that "disillusionment is most often the child of illusion." Starting out with the wrong set of expectations sets you up for disappointment. These sermons never claimed to be exhaustive or definitive statements about childhood, adolescence, adulthood or agedness. They are, at best, suggestive descriptions of what life is like at each of these junctions, some of the growth-challenges that one can expect to face, and particular resources that the Christian gospel makes available to enhance these times in our lives.

My hopes are modest: first, to provide an individual with perspective on his or her own past, insight into his or her own present, and preparation for his or her own future; and second, to provide an individual some "handles of understanding" in what is going on in the lives of family and friends who are at these various stages along life's way. A veritable explosion of material has been published since this was written which h as a ugmented a nd e nlarged t hese c hapters. The fact that Gail Sheehy's volume *Passages* was a number-one best-seller for weeks is but one sign that our culture has been anxious to know more about the challenges of the afternoon and evening of life.

Sam Keene once described a wise person as one "who knows what time it is in his or her life." My highest hope is that some of these words will contribute to the growth of that kind of wisdom.

John R. Claypool

CHAPTER ONE

CHILDHOOD

CHILDHOOD

ANOINTED WITH DELIGHT

For all our individual differences, each one of us begins the saga of our lives in exactly the same way—through the trauma of being separated from a warm and secure place in another's body to having to exist on our own as individuals. At first our condition is one of almost total helplessness and dependence, but gradually two important growth-challenges begin to develop, the consequences of which can vary widely depending upon how they are handled.

The first of these has to do with the issue of personal worth and how the child comes to regard his or her existence in the world. I think it is safe to say that this becomes the number one item on the agenda when a little creature is thrust out of the womb into this new arena. Although the question is certainly not formulated in rational terms, nonetheless the whole organism begins to wonder: "Where am I now? In what kind of context do I find myself? Will my needs be met here as adequately as they were in my mother's womb?" Then comes the most urgent question of all: "How am I regarded in this place? Is it good that I am here? Is my presence valued and welcomed or deplored and resented?" These are the issues that probably dominate the dawning consciousness of a newborn child, and from the very first moment, signals start moving back and forth between "the big people" and the little one that begin to answer the value-question. Every facet of the relationship is significant here—the words that are spoken, the tone of voice, the way the child is held, the emotional mood of the whole atmosphere that surrounds this new beginning. Here the process of constructing a self-image begins, and fortunate is the child who encounters positive affection early in life.

Same Keene was one such child. As he was visiting with his father just before the older man died, he had occasion to look back over their life together and thank his father for the excellent job he had done. "You have always been there whenever any of us children needed you and, across the years, you have given us the best single gift that any parent could give—*you took delight in us*. In all sorts of ways you let us know that you were glad we were here, that we had value in your eyes, that our presence was a joy and not a burden to you."

When I read those words, I recalled something that Gordon Cosby once wrote which surprised me very much at the time. He said that the first and foremost responsibility of parents was *to enjoy their children*. Given my Puritan heritage, with its emphasis always on the "oughts" and "shoulds," I was startled to hear the words "enjoy" and "responsibility" in the same sentence. However, upon reflection, I could not agree more. Nothing can secure children more fully in this new world than knowing their personhood brings delight to their parents.

Is not this the way Genesis described God's reaction

to the creation God had just birthed into being? God looked at what God had made and was utterly pleased with it. Things were far from finished or perfected at that point, but nonetheless, the One who had created all things took delight in everything that One had created. Such unconditional affection is the foundation on which all positive self-esteem is built.

Yet, having made that point emphatically, let me now add two provisos. First, this gift of delight that is so important must be received and internalized by the child just as decisively as it has to be given. Also, the gift of delight can come from persons other than one's biological parents. Obviously, the mother and father are in the best position to give a positive message to their child, for they have the initial, foundational contact with him or her, and I am sure this is God's intention. But even if these individuals fail, or simply do a poor job, all is not lost, for the God of the Bible always has a "backup system" to the primary instrumentalities. What I am saying is that I believe God intends for every child to be exposed to some form of delight during those formative years, even though it may not come through the normal channels.

Childhood: Anointed with Delight

This may have been young David's experience, it seems to me. Over a hundred pages in the Old Testament tell about this remarkable human being, but we know less about his early childhood than any other part of his life. We do know that he was the youngest of ten children, having seven brothers and two sisters, and there are some grounds for believing that he was hardly a favored child among them. Do you remember the account where old Samuel came to Bethlehem and announced that God had prepared for Israel a new king from among the sons of a certain Jesse (1 Samuel 16:1-13)? When the father was told of this possibility, it did not occur to him that David might be the chosen one. Jesse had older and more handsome sons than the baby of the family; and when Samuel asked to see the members of David's family, the older boys were the ones his father presented. Even Samuel was infected momentarily by this beauty-contest approach to establishing human worth, but God challenged that fact by stating: "Humans look on the outward appearance, but I look on the heart" (1 Samuel 16:7).

Young David was actually God's choice, and, to the amazement of the whole family, he was called in from the fields and anointed then and there by Samuel as a person of special worth and destiny in the eyes of Yahweh. The important thing to note here is that David, who had been overlooked by his natural parents, received this gift of delight when it was offered him, even though it did not come through his own parents. This experience with Samuel and the Lord God must have helped David to develop a positive self-image apart from what his mother and father had done or failed to do. The Scriptures say that "the Spirit of the Lord possessed David mightily" (1 Samuel 16:13) through the affirmation of Samuel, and he was flexible enough to take delight wherever he could get it and build his life accordingly.

It is important to realize that the task of helping a child come to a sense of positive worth does not fall on any one person exclusively. The parents cannot accomplish this process all by themselves, no matter how effectively they love, if the child refuses to accept and internalize the sense of delight that is being offered. By the same token, neither can a child come to a positive opinion about himself or herself all alone. The sense of delight must be consciously and deliberately both given and received; and if there is openness on all sides, I have faith that God will find a person to give the gift of delight to a child—if not the natural parents, then perhaps an uncle or a grandparent or a Sunday school teacher or a friend or someone. It is basic to the Christian religion that we should always be willing to do "compensatory work" when the natural processes of life have broken down. By the same token, no one has the right to assume total self-pity or blame his self-despising on the failure of this or that adult. To be sure, it is a handicap to have parents who cannot or will not give the gift of delight. Yet, if one is flexible enough to receive the gift from whomever it may come, I believe there will always be a Samuel to compensate for the failures of the family.

The words that Jesus heard as He came up from His baptism are precisely the message God wants to communicate to every one of us—"This is My beloved Child, in whom I am well pleased. This is My son or daughter in whom I take delight" (Matthew 3:17). Getting this message through and internalized in the depth of being is the first challenge of childhood. As parents and friends, we should be diligent to beam this message as clearly and as widely as we can. As children, we must be as open and as flexible as possible t o however this gift of delight might come.

Another important challenge is helping children to realize the gifts they have within them and calling them to become responsible stewards of these powers. As important as a sense of self-worth may be, it is only the first step, for with it must come a vision of destiny, a realization that one was created for a purpose and that all one's gifts were meant to become presents for someone else. Thus, a child needs to be given what I call "a Christmas-Tree Spirit" about himself or herself; that is, he needs someone to point out "the packages" that are part of one's nature and to encourage h im o r h er t o u nwrap a nd d iscover a nd develop these capacities. This had obviously been done for David, perhaps more effectively than self-esteem had been developed. At an early age, he was already out in the fields, involved in the family enterprise.

The notion that something was being expected of David, not just given to him, accounts for his becoming such an outgoing, effective person later on. Early in his life, someone helped David come to the realization that he possessed tremendous gifts which were needed by the world and encouraged him to unwrap these gifts and start giving them away. Out of this kind of expectation came the musician, the poet, the athlete, the warrior, and the capable ruler who so blessed Israel. Expectation was added to affirmation and acceptance—a combination that helps a child to move successfully into life.

Years ago, Dr. James Dobson wrote an excellent little book called *Hide or Seek* on the subject of building authentic self-esteem in our children. In addition to providing them unconditional emotional acceptance, Dobson says that we must help our children recognize their special skills and inspire them to develop them. He feels that our "superstar culture" is very unfair and arbitrary in the way it reserves affirmation for only the exceptionally beautiful and unusually brilliant, but he points out that this is not likely to change overnight. Therefore, we do our children a great disservice if we allow them to grow up without helping them explore themselves and develop some kind of competence that can give them a sense of satisfaction in the world.

Dobson related his own experience of growing up.

Because of his slight physical build, it soon became apparent that he was not going to be able to compete successfully in football or basketball. However, his father sensed that tennis was a game for which he did have aptitude, so he urged him to learn to play that game. Dobson said that, at first, he resented having to leave the sandpile to begin to hit balls back and forth across a net; but before long, his gift began to emerge and he started finding real satisfaction in being a good tennis player. Thus, by the time he got to high school, he had an athletic skill to compensate for not being able to play contact sports. This is just one illustration of how helping our children recognize the powers that they do possess can aid in the unfolding of their lives.

In our kind of culture, simply to let children drift into adolescence without any developed competence can prove disastrous. I once heard Charles Campbell of the Federal Correctional Institute in Fort Worth say that the great majority of the people in our penal institutions were not so much bad as they were inept. Never having developed any skill that enabled them to function creatively in our society, they had nothing that gave them satisfaction or was of worth to the culture. The importance of this facet of the childhood challenge cannot be overlooked. No matter how secure a child may feel in the delight of his or her family, no matter how much self-worth may have been internalized, if he or she has not also developed a sense of responsibility to take what has been given and pass it on to others, then it is not likely that God's dream for that child can ever come true.

Here then, it seems to me, is the nature of this segment of life called childhood, its unique challenges, and the Good News of God as it applies to this point in the journey. The crucial areas of concern have to do with the issues of worth and gifts. For parents, the challenges involve giving the gifts of delight as widely as we can—to our own children, to be sure, but to all the children we meet. For children, it means receiving the gift, however it may come. Not every biological parent can or will give his or her children a sense of delight, but God is not so easily defeated. God has a boundless reservoir of positive feelings for each one of us, and if we are flexible and sensitive enough, God will find some Samuel to anoint us with "compensatory grace." There is also the challenge of expectation to impart to our children—a sense of responsibility for the gifts they possess. By the grace of God, they both *are* something special and can *do* something special. Expectation without acceptance is a frightening thing, for it is overly demanding and becomes a dehumanizing kind of legalism. However, acceptance without expectation is just as bad, for it leaves unfulfilled the great potential within a child.

David was blessed by both acceptance and expectation. He was "anointed with delight" and made to feel he had something important to do in history. A magnificent life was built upon these twin foundations. Can we do less than learn from his example, and in our own lives, go and do likewise?

CHAPTER TWO

ADOLESCENCE

ADOLESCENCE

THE VALLEY OF TRANSITION

James Dobson has described the segment of the human pilgrimage called adolescence as a "time of indigestion, heartburn and trauma." He says it is hard to tell for whom it is the most difficult—the adolescent who is undergoing all kinds of physical and emotional and social upheavals, or the other members of the family who suddenly realize that this child is not a baby any longer and must now begin to face independently some of the challenges of life. Dobson concludes that adolescence is a time of life "that offers something painful for everybody."

43

I think this assessment of Dobson's is essentially correct. While every stage of life has its own particular challenges and turbulence, the traumas of adolescence may well be the most intense of all. It is all the more imperative that no one just "happen upon" this period unprepared. The dictum that runs throughout this whole book—*what we do not know most assuredly can hurt us*—is nowhere truer than in that difficult transitional period called adolescence.

Several years ago, while I was pastor in Kentucky, I received through the mail a packet containing a little book entitled *Understanding Womanhood*, along with one of the most poignant letters I have ever read. It came from a couple in the northern part of that state who had only one child—a lovely little girl who was the apple of their eye. They had attempted to give her every material and educational advantage, yet unexpectedly, just as she turned thirteen, she put a gun in her mouth and committed suicide. After her death, they found the diary she had been keeping and, for the first time, they realized that she had been experiencing great inner turmoil about the changes that were occurring in her body, her feelings and all around her. You see, no one had forewarned her about all the things that start happening to a girl around twelve or thirteen, and the fearfulness of it all was too much for her to handle.

The letter went on to say that the couple had decided to take the money that they had saved up for their child's college education and send a copy of this book to every clergyman in Kentucky. It ended touchingly: "If we had only known and had been able to communicate to our little daughter some of the truths that are in this book, perhaps she would be with us yet."

When I put down the letter, I realized how relevant was Jesus' prayer from the cross: "Father, forgive them, for they know not what they do." Think of the pain that has occurred across the years, not from human badness, but from human blindness! What those parents, and, consequently, that little girl did not know about adolescence did hurt them.

I do not mean to imply that any amount of light will automatically make this segment of the journey easy or painless. However, it cannot but help to know as much as we can about that "valley of the shadows" between childhood and adulthood called adolescence.

The first thing we need to get straight is the meaning of the term itself. The word, *adolescence*, does not refer to the awakening of sexual awareness in the individual. The technical term for that is puberty. Adolescence stands for the transitional period between the dependency of childhood and the independency—or more accurately, the interdependency—of adulthood. Its length has varied from culture to culture. In many primitive tribes, there was no adolescent period at all. When the time was right, a boy who one day was playing without responsibility and under the complete control of his parents, would be sent that night on a symbolic hunt; and if he survived, he was regarded thereafter as an adult member of the tribe.

In our Western industrialized civilizations, however, we have developed the longest period of adolescence in history. It can last for as much as fifteen years in some cases. I know several graduate students in their twenties who are still being supported by their parents. While they are physically and emotionally adults, they are still adolescents in terms of dependency. Obviously, this is an "in-between" time, a segment of life when an individual is denied the privileges of childhood and yet does not possess the freedom and power of adulthood either.

It is not surprising, therefore, that all kinds of pressures and conflicts surface. In the most literal sense, one encounters "growing pains." Both the adolescent and the family members are faced with something new; that is, they must learn to let a relationship that has existed in one basic form for a decade or so begin to stretch and enlarge without snapping or exploding.

How can the intimacy that human beings have known as parent and child be transformed into the kind of intimacy that is appropriate for adults with adults? This is the challenge that the period of adolescence flings down before us, and it takes very different forms for the various parties involved.

For example, the growth-task facing the parent is the delicate feat of letting up on the relationship without letting go of it completely. The adolescent very much needs for the parent to step back and give space enough so that he or she can begin to make decisions on his or her own. A teenager once complained: "My mother hovers over me like a helicopter. I'm fifteen years old, yet if I'm in the basement and sneeze and she is in the attic, she turns into a distance runner and is by my side the next moment saying breathlessly: 'Are you catching a cold?'" There was a time in that boy's infancy when such attentiveness was absolutely crucial to his survival, but now a measure of distance is just as essential. Not total distance, however— remember, while the adolescent is no longer a dependent child, neither is he or she a fully autonomous or capable adult either. To step back while not walking out on a relationship altogether is a difficult balance to achieve and, for the parent, learning how to distance one's self appropriately from the adolescent is a formidable new growth-challenge.

For the adolescent, the challenge can also be put in terms of distance, but of an utterly different form. He or she must learn to pick up what the parents are laying down, learn to accept responsibility increasingly for his or her own decisions and support, learn the secret of his or her own gifts and the ways of the world, and develop the ability to walk into the larger arena of relationships without walking away from the sources that brought him or her into the world. The goal is not independence so much as interdependency—coming to relate, adult to adult, not only with one's peers, but also with one's parents. Let us repeat the challenges: in the one case, to let up without letting go, to step back without walking out on a relationship and in the other, to pick up responsibility and walk forward into the world without walking away from one's sources. Nobody ever said it would be easy, and to my knowledge no family or person has ever carried it off perfectly—not even King David, remarkable human being that he was.

The whole seventeenth chapter of 1 Samuel describes a climactic moment in the drama of David's adolescence. He was obviously at an in-between stage. He was no longer playing in the sandpile out back, but rather out in the fields tending sheep. However, he was still under the control of other adults—his father and subsequently Saul the King. Three of his brothers had enlisted with Saul to fight the Philistines, and one day David's father suggested that David take them some food and bring back word of their welfare.

When David arrived at the battle station, he was dismayed to find the forces of Israel quaking in fear. A huge mountain of a man named Goliath came out from the other side every morning and evening and challenged any Hebrew to engage in one-to-one combat. There had been a day when Saul the King would have risen to such a challenge in a moment, but his courage and confidence had left him, and as a result, the whole Hebrew army was being debilitated with fear.

David's reaction was a classic expression of adolescent idealism. He came into that situation unjaded and unfatigued by life, which is one of the great roles that youths play in the process of history. He had not "been everywhere and seen everything and done it all." He had an exuberant faith in the God of Israel and great confidence in his own abilities. Thus, to everyone's amazement, this shepherd boy offered to accept Goliath's challenge and fight for the honor of the Lord of Hosts!

When word of this boldness got back to Saul, he sent for the young man. What follows is a classic interaction between an emerging adolescent and the older generation. Saul's first reaction was surprise; it startled him that a lad who so shortly before had been playing underfoot would now be making "man-noises" and proposing to do something significant. (It is easy to freeze our children sentimentally in the baby category, so that almost invariably their emergence as significant individuals catches us by surprise. However, it is wise not to undermine the idealism of adolescents.) David countered the charge that he was merely a child by telling of having fought lions and bears out in the wilds as a shepherd, until finally it dawned on Saul that the one before him was not a baby any longer, but a young man come of age.

Saul's next reaction was also typical. Realizing David meant business and was ready to go out and fight Goliath, he proceeded to load him down with his own armor—to take the shields and breastplates that had been designed for him and put them on David. This must have been a comical spectacle indeed. Saul was reputedly a very large man, standing head and shoulders above the average Hebrew. Just imagine how young David must have looked in all that oversized get-up! He could not even move, much less fight. Yet is not this precisely what we parents do when it finally hits us that our children are going to have to move on unaccompanied by us? Don't we hurriedly try to dress them up in our ideas, our advice about this and that, what we did on our first date or in high school or so forth?

What we do not realize is that they are unique individuals living in a different time from our past; somebody else's armor does not fit nor is it really what they need. Every person must forge his or her own weapons and beliefs and convictions.

In speaking of children in *The Prophet*, Kahil Gibran very wisely says to parents: "You may give them your love, but not your thoughts, for they have their own thoughts. You may house their bodies, but not their souls, for their souls dwell in the house of tomorrow, which you cannot visit, not even in your dreams. You may strive to be like them, but seek not to make them like you, for life goes not backwards nor tarries with yesterday. You are the bow from which your children as living arrows are sent forth. The Archer sees the mark upon the path of the Infinite, and He bends you with His might that His arrows may go swift and far. Let your bending in the Archer's hand be for gladness, for even as He loves the arrow that flies, so he loves the bow that is stable." This is so true, and David reminded Saul of that as politely as he could.

History is not a treadmill, nor is one individual a carbon copy of another. We can give our children a certain feel for life, a sense of what is right and wrong. We can "train them up in the way they should go;" that is, we can point them in the right direction, but when it comes to the specific armor they will need, it is not our sacred responsibility, but theirs, to fit themselves with it.

David had obviously done his adolescent growth-work rather thoroughly before this moment. For example, religion was not a secondhand tradition as far as he was concerned. He had obviously come to terms very personally with Yahweh. He had moved from the "what-I've-been-taught" stage to the "what-I-believe" stage, and this only occurs when one is encouraged "to ask and to seek and to knock." If we adults fall in a faint the first time a teenager expresses doubt or begins to search, we hinder the very processes that lead eventually to mature faith. This is a point where "letting up" on indoctrination and stepping back to make room for growth is essential.

David had also begun to know himself—he recognized the shape of his individuality and its boundaries. He had tested his skills in the give-and-take of life. Long before this moment, his parents had begun to remove their protective shell and allowed him to go to work and face the wilds of the desert. In that process, he had come to understand something of what the world out there was like and how he himself was equipped to cope with it. Thus, in that moment before the King, David did what every adolescent has to do—he took responsibility for his own life and asked for the right to meet a challenge with his own resources and ingenuity.

Here is the climactic moment in this high drama of adolescence—the point at which the young person has the courage "to leave father and mother" and walk forward on his own toward the giant called life, and the parents have the courage to let the beloved one go with only the sling and staff of his own choosing. It is hard to say which of these two challenges requires the most courage. It is certainly not easy for any of those involved. Just imagine what must have been going through David's mind as he stepped out there alone before that nine-and-a-half-foot monster. And how must Saul and David's brothers have felt as they watched David move into that ravine?

"The valley of the shadows of adolescence" is scary, but we might as well face the fact that *there is no way around it!* David never could have become the adult he became apart from this kind of experience. All parties concerned functioned well in this moment, and it became a building block for the legendary career that was to follow. The relationship between David and his sources stretched and expanded that day without snapping or exploding. The intimacy appropriate to childhood grew into a different kind of intimacy—that of an interdependent adult with adults. David had the courage to take the responsibility for his own existence from his parents, but as he walked forward into the world, he did not walk away from a continuing relationship with his family of origin. He remembered that he was able to see as far as he could because he was standing on the shoulders and the accomplishments of his sources.

By the same token, his parents and Saul had the

courage to let up without letting go of David altogether. They stepped back at the appropriate time, but they did not walk out on the relationship completely. This is essential, for adolescence is more than one dramatic experience which will not be repeated once it is over. Usually it involves a series of forays into the adult world from which one then comes back wounded and bleeding, in need of healing and reassurance.

Not every adolescent does as well against the giants of the world as David did. Jesus told once of a younger son whose decision to launch out on his own proved disastrous (Luke 15:11-24). Unlike David, this young man had not done his homework: he did not know himself or the world, and he wound up losing everything in the far country. His first reaction was to run home and try to climb back into the womb. He had had his fill of freedom. What he wanted now was the security of being a hired servant, of having someone else make all the decisions for him. Luckily for him, the father who had let up and stepped back had not let go or walked out on his son completely. When the lad came limping home, defeated by life, the father refused to let him re-enter dependency. He showed him great compassion, but then called for a robe and a ring and some shoes, symbols of the responsibility and adulthood to which this son was called. In other words, the father's parenting tasks continued long after the adolescent left for the first time, and this is how it should be.

Alan Paton summarized the stance of the parent beautifully in these words: "I see my son wearing long trousers; I tremble at this. I see he goes forward confidently, he does not know so fully his own gentleness. Go forward, eager and reverent child. See here, I begin to take my hands away from you. I shall see you walk carelessly on the edge of the precipice, but if you wish, you shall hear no word come out of me. My whole soul will be sick with apprehension, but I shall not disobey you. Life sees you coming, she sees you come with assurance toward her. She lies in wait for you. She cannot but hurt you. Yet go forward. Go forward. I hold the bandages and the ointment ready. And if you would go elsewhere and lie alone with your wounds, I shall not intrude upon you. If you would seek the help of some other person, I will not come forcing myself upon you. If you should fall into sin, innocent one, that is the way of this pilgrimage.

Struggle against it, not for one fraction of a moment concede its dominion. It will occasion you grief and sorrow, it will torment you. But hate not God, nor turn from Him in shame or self-reproach. He has seen many such, and His compassion is as great as His creation. Be tempted and fall and return. Return and be tempted and fall, a thousand times a thousand, even to a thousand thousand. For out of this tribulation there comes a peace, deep in the soul and surer than any dream."

In the end, it is that hope which illumines this valley of transition called adolescence. "Out of this tribulation" can come a peace, a wholeness, a magnificent human being like David. As James Dobson pointed out, there is something painful for everybody in this time of indigestion, heartburn, and trauma. Yet it can be endured; "yea, the valley of the shadow of adolescence" can be walked *through* to the light of the other side! However, let us not forget that in order to do so, everybody involved faces a challenge. For the parents, it is learning to let up without letting go, to step back without walking out on the relationship. For the adolescent it is learning to pick up what is being laid down, and to walk forward without walking away from one's sources. Stretching and expanding a relationship so that everything becomes bigger, without snapping or exploding the bond—that is the challenge adolescence poses for us all. May God give us courage, like David's long ago, to face this particular challenge, and by His grace to continue to grow.

So let it be!

CHAPTER THREE

ADULTHOOD

ADULTHOOD

UP AND DOWN THE MOUNTAIN

I sometimes wish I had never heard that familiar formula that comes at the climax of so many fairy tales: "And they lived happily ever after." As a rule, everything leading up to these words is colored by conflict and struggle. Dragons have to be fought, curses broken, and all kinds of effort exerted. Then suddenly, out of all the world, Prince Charming and Sleeping Beauty find each other, and the atmosphere changes radically. It is like coming out of a choppy sea into an utterly tranquil port, for the rest of life is described in that idyllic image—"and they lived happily ever after."

The reason I am sorry I heard so much about this as a child is that it distorted my expectations of what adulthood was going to be like. It gave me the illusion that the "morning of life" was the time of turbulence, and that once a person had finished his or her education, chosen a vocation, selected a mate, and settled down, all would be serene and placid thereafter. The hassles of having to grow and change and decide were supposedly all behind a person at that point. However, the truth of the matter is that nothing could be further from actual experience. These six words are really a fairy tale in the most literal sense. Think of the people who have been crippled with disappointment and disillusionment because they thought adulthood was going to be one kind of experience and it turned out to be another!

I would have been far better off if I had gotten my "feel for life" from the Bible rather than from fairy tales, for God's Book never fosters the illusion that life gets easy at some point or that the challenge to grow comes to an end. Jesus said: "In the world, you shall have tribulation" (John 16:33). He did not restrict this statement to childhood or adolescence; it is a description of the whole human pilgrimage. Such realism is not to be confused with pessimism, however. Jesus went on to say: "Be of good cheer; I have overcome the world." He means that, while He does not promise to deliver us *out* of tribulation, struggle and the need to grow, but rather to show us how to cope with all this and enable us to be "more than conquerors" of our circumstances, rather than conquered by them.

As we turn now to the largest single segment of the human journey—adulthood—this is the point I want to emphasize. It is not the time of life when automatically and effortlessly we begin to "live happily ever after." In terms of both pressures and possibilities, it is the most strenuous segment of our existence. If adolescence is the most *intense* stage along the way, I would say adulthood is the most *demanding*. Not only is it so long, but it involves many different challenges simultaneously. Gail Sheehy has coined the phrase "concomitant growth" to describe the unique challenge of adulthood, and I believe she is correct. It means continuing to grow concurrently on the three basic frontiers of adulthood:

65

work or vocation, relationships with one's "significant others," and one's own unique selfhood. Let's face it—this is quite a challenge indeed. Have you ever known an adult who handled all of it perfectly?

The great temptation here is to become unbalanced, to give the vast majority of one's energies to only one of these areas and neglect the other two. Gail Sheehy tells of a forty-six-year-old TV newscaster who had climbed to the top of his profession and was basking in the affluence and affirmation that went with being a national celebrity. However, he was not as satisfied or fulfilled as one might suppose he would be. He commented one day: "I am near the top of the mountain that I saw as a young man, but lo and behold, this is not snow up here, it is mostly salt." He said most of the persons he knew who were considered "successful" had left their personal lives far behind them. Professionally, they were terrific, but on a personal level their lives were in utter disarray. What has happened, he notes, is that these individuals quit growing relationally and personally somewhere between the ages of twelve and fourteen when the crying ambition to succeed overwhelmed them, but now that they are looking out from "the top of the heap," a whole new agenda emerges.

Going down the mountain is quite a different art from climbing up it. Where, asked that celebrity, are the navigational charts for descent, the kinds of relationships that will sustain a person in the afternoon and evening of life? This is a classic example of what happens to someone who has worked on only one growth front during much of his or her adulthood. This man was feeling great loneliness and personal emptiness because work and concern with succeeding professionally had dominated his whole existence.

Failure at "concomitant growth" may sound like a modern phenomenon, but it is not: three thousand years ago, David did the very same thing with his adulthood, and the consequences which resulted from such imbalance were mixed, to say the least.

On the one hand, like that TV newscaster, David "made it big" professionally. In fact, it was incredible how in five short decades he rose from the obscurity of tending sheep to be the uncontested ruler from the Nile to the Euphrates. Such success was attributable to many factors, of course, but basic to it all was David's remarkable ability to concentrate on doing something rather than just being something.

I shall never forget the time I first heard that distinction made. A personnel manager of a national firm said this was the thing he tried to determine initially about any new executive trainee. He described the person who wanted to be something as one whose ego needs were still dominant in his or her existence. Thus, at every juncture, this one would be asking: "How can I use this situation to enhance my personhood and position?" This kind of person, he said, "will always have blurred vision, will never be able to risk anything or sacrifice, and thus would be a liability in the higher echelons of decision-making." However, the person who wants essentially "to do something" had his or her ego needs met healthily. This one can look at a difficult situation with a clear focus and ask simply: "What needs to be done here?" This kind of person can risk and sacrifice, and will be worth millions more to the company throughout his or her career than the person who always strives "to be something."

The secret to David's great professional success lies right at this point—he was consistently the kind of person who wanted to do something rather than be something. He did not have to waste energy bolstering his own ego or acting spitefully. Getting on with the task of making Israel a great nation was foremost on his agenda and, again and again, this priority enabled him to do the strategic thing.

For example, King Saul treated David most unfairly for many years. David was never anything but a loyal and helpful subject, but the king's insecurity led him to harass David unmercifully. Yet when Saul and his son were killed in battle, David did not rub his hands together gleefully and say: "It serves the old scoundrel right." Along with all of Israel, David went into genuine mourning. Eventually, this lack of vindictiveness led the northern tribes who were close to Saul to ask David to rule them as well. When this happened, David made another strategic move. He could have made his headquarters in Hebron the new capital, and thus ground in the tribes of the north that he had won out over them; but this would have been an ego trip for his benefit alone, not a move to unify the country. So instead, David conquered a Jebusite stronghold called Jerusalem, which the Israelites had never controlled before, and he made this neutral site the center of his new beginnings.

One of David's greatest strengths was that he had moved from the infantile need to have everything serve him to the maturity of genuinely wanting to serve others. Psychologists identify this attitude as one of the distinguishing marks of maturity: the point at which we cease to be preoccupied with what parent-figures can do for us and decide to become parent-figures and mentors ourselves, caring for, blessing and guiding other people. Erik Erikson calls it "generativity," and without it no person really comes to the fulfillment of life. All of us start out in utter dependence, but woe unto us if that is where we remain all of our days! This does not mean everyone must have a career or engage in some professional activity, but it does mean that in our adulthood, some way, somehow, we should become part of the answer instead of part of the problem by contributing something positive to the stream of history.

David is a real model for us at the pont of generativity and of making a difference in the world by giving himself. This aspect of his life was great. The problem was that there was not concomitant growth on the other frontiers at the same time. For when we turn to a consideration of the rest of his life, it becomes evident that David's overinvestment in the area of work led to tragic neglect in the other facets of his existence.

Take, for example, the area of family or significant other persons. If an individual is determined to be a workaholic, as David turned out to be, it appears that he or she would choose not to take on the responsibilities of establishing personal intimacy. Tragically enough, this is rarely the case. More often than not, people like David involve themselves heavily in relationships, and then create wastelands of neglect. For example, it does not appear that David ever worked through one of the primary tasks of adulthood, namely, establishing a relation of authentic intimacy with another person. He had many wives but no deep relationships and, as a result, he grew lonelier and lonelier as the years went by. It is much easier to substitute several superficial relationships instead of building even one intimate relationship in life, but the outcome is not the same. Infected by our trade-in, throw-away mentality, the TV newscaster I mentioned earlier had gone from wife to wife in his climb up the ladder. Every time this man and his mate encountered difficulty, instead of using the occasion to deepen and strengthen their bond, he slid off sidewise and established another superficial alliance.

From what we can tell in 1 and 2 Samuel, this is what David did as well, and he encountered the inevitable end of that pattern of relating—utter and awesome loneliness. The TV celebrity really wanted some companionship as he started down the mountain, but the way in which he had used his relationship powers held little promise. By his own admission, he had never put much of himself into that side of life, and as the Bible says: "He who soweth sparingly shall reap sparingly" (2 Corinthians 9:6). David came up short in the same way, and he grew lonelier and lonelier.

There is something for us all to learn here: it takes genuine effort and persistence to establish an authentic intimate relationship with anyone. Neither good marriages nor, for that matter, even deep friendships are made in heaven. They may be designed there, but the work of constructing them is done on earth. Only those who are willing to stay with the long-range task of faithful relationship-building will avoid the loneliness that was recognized long ago as not good for any human being.

David's failure in the area of intimacy includes his relationships with his children as well. He had lots of them, to be sure; the Bible lists at least nineteen sons and there is no telling how many daughters. From the way they later fought, connived and betrayed each other, it seems clear that from the beginning they had little contact with or guidance from their famous father. To use Gail Sheehy's term, there was no concomitant growth on the relational frontier of David's life. He zoomed way out in professional competence, but at the expense of the people closest to him. I imagine that as David looked back over his life from the perspective of old age, this particular imbalance of overinvestment and neglect caused him considerable pain.

It is also fairly obvious from the record that David put forth very little effort in cultivating his own inwardness and uniqueness as a person. Lewis Sherrill says that, while preoccupation with self is a weakness in adolescents, developing a healthy sense of oneself becomes an essential task in adulthood. Having a coherent view of life and coming to terms with the uniqueness of one's individuality are very important. Oscar Wilde once wrote, "It is tragic how few people ever possess their own souls before they die. 'Nothing is more rare in any man,' says Emerson, 'than an act of his own.' It is quite true. Most people are other people. Their thoughts are someone else's opinions. Their lives are a mimicry and their passions a quotation."

I have seen person after person who had let someone else decide everything for them for so long that when they were asked, "What would *you* like to do?" they have no answer. Having been programmed externally for so long, they have no earthly idea. Did you know that more suicides occur on Saturday and Sunday than all the other days of the week put together? The reason for this "week-end psychosis" is clear. When life has been structured by someone else all week and, suddenly, the individual is left to decide things for himself, many are so unskilled in "listening to their innermost thoughts" or answering the voice of their uniqueness that they crumble under the pressure.

Adulthood: Up and Down the Mountain

One spring David did not go to battle as he had been doing for years and years. With the structure of external habits removed, he did not know what to do with himself. It was during such a period that he saw Bathsheba from his rooftop and set in motion a train of events that proved disastrous for all concerned.

The cultivation and care of one's own interior being is utterly important lest we grow old in great emptiness. When Jesus challenged His disciples to "bear much fruit," this is part of what He meant—to get in touch with all that is within us and begin to bring forth the treasurers of that uniqueness. As we have seen, David had done a better job of growing outwardly than inwardly. He had neglected the cultivation of his own individuality, and the result was sad indeed.

The challenge, then, is to concomitant growth, simultaneous development in the spheres of work and relationship and selfhood. Herein lies the great growth-challenges of adulthood—generativity, intimacy, and self-fulfillment; and, I repeat, that this is by no means an easy task for anyone. Not even David—legendary figure that he was—managed to achieve this balance. Like so many before and after him, he overinvested himself in work to the exclusion of family relations or personal self-realization. I have known others to get just as much out of balance by overinvesting in family life or "doing their own thing" to the exclusion of work. One thing is obvious—real life is not like the fairy tales. There are no points beyond which struggle and growth are not needed.

We will live happily ever after only to the degree that we take the ideal of concomitant growth seriously and keep on working all our days at the tasks of generativity, intimacy, and self-realization. To exclude any one of these leads to distortion and incompleteness. For most adults, this is at least a forty-year enterprise. May God help us not to waste a single day or leave out any one of these important tasks!

CHAPTER FOUR

SENIOR ADULTHOOD

SENIOR ADULTHOOD

FOCUS ON BEING

This chapter marks the last leg of an important journey. Our original intention was to attempt to sketch out a road map of this human pilgrimage in which we all find ourselves. What is it like to be a child, an adolescent, an adult, and finally an aged person? For all of our individual uniquenesses, there are certain predictable characteristics and challenges in each of these segments, and our underlying assumption has been "the more light, the better." Here again, as we have found earlier, what we do not know most assuredly can hurt us!

At no point in this process have I attempted to hold myself up as an expert in these matters. I am as much a learner and a fellow struggler as any of you. However, I must confess that I am less comfortable at this juncture of our study than at any other point, for the obvious reason that I am dealing with something that I have only begun to experience firsthand. Up to now, I have had more existential knowledge to go on, for I have experienced what it is like to be a child and an adolescent and a young and median adult, but I am only in the early stages of the phenomenon of agedness. I am just beginning to know firsthand what it feels like to have one's physical powers diminish. Just this year, I retired from full-time work in ministry after more than fifty years, to part-time work or semi-retirement; and I have not yet noticed an increasing number of my contemporaries passing away into the mystery of death. Therefore, I want to acknowledge this limitation at the outset and confess that I write as a novice at this last stage of life.

Let me also acknowledge, however, that I have been fortunate in having some great mentors to guide me in this area. My work has given me the opportunity to share deeply with lots of people as they negotiate "the evening of life." My own mother lived to be 93, and my father lived to be 100, so I learned volumes from watching the way they aged with grace. Then too, I have been most blessed to have served as a colleague with Dr. Franklin Segler during my days at Broadway Church. He taught me much about this period of life, both through the fine little book he wrote on the subject and, more importantly, by the way he himself handled this stage of life so creatively.

In terms of what happens to one physically and vocationally and relationally, senior adulthood represents "new ground" and poses a full set of brand-new growth-challenges. However, the other side of that coin is that we are preparing all through our lives for the time of agedness, whether we realize that fact or not.

One of the main lessons I have learned from this study is the vast interconnectedness of life. The way a person handles the challenges at one period of his or her existence directly affects all that is to follow. Thus, in a very real sense, we begin laying the foundations for our agedness as far back as childhood, and the segment of life we are talking about now represents the culmination of how well or how poorly we have done our growth-work at earlier stages. I do not want to be misunderstood here: I firmly believe that genuine change is possible at every stage along the way of life. It is never too late nor is one ever too old to alter radically the shape of one's existence. Still, the truth of the matter is that what we become in agedness is a culmination of the choices and habits we have developed in childhood, adolescence and adult-hood.

This was certainly the case with King David, the man whose life saga we have been studying throughout this journey. I was interested to find two distinctly different accounts of the last stage of David's life. In 1 Chronicles (29:26-28) there is a later, rather idealized version of this period. The great religious piety of David is emphasized, and one would assume from this account that the final hours and the transition of power from David to Solomon were easy and automatic.

In 1 Kings, however, a very difference picture is painted. The kinds of struggle that had characterized all of David's reign continued. For example, it was by no means simple to settle the issue of succession. (It never is when great wealth and power are involved.) Absalom had been "the apple of his father's eye." As David's first-born son he was the logical heir to the throne, but, as you may remember, Absalom did not know how to wait. Reaching for the crown prematurely, he tried to take by force what would have eventually been given to him, and in the battle that ensued, he was killed. Later, when it became evident that David was very weak and about to die, Adonijah, the next son chronologically, did the same thing Absalom had done. Traveling to the northern section of Israel, he proclaimed himself as the king and attempted to take the crown from his father's head. He was joined in this effort by Joab, the head of the military establishment, and Abiathar, the high priest and leader of the Temple.

No sooner did this happen, however, than the prophet Nathan stepped into the power struggle. He was the one, remember, who had stood up to David years before concerning his treatment of Bathsheba and Uriah the Hittite. Now he apprised the aged king of what was happening and reminded him of a promise he had made Bathsheba in light of the pain he had brought into her life. The child conceived of their initial affair had died, but later on, after Bathsheba had become David's wife, she had borne him another son named Solomon. This was the child to succeed David, in Nathan's judgment, for Solomon, who never had been a warrior like his father, had a brilliant mind and was obviously the best equipped of all David's children to do the things that needed to be done next in the Kingdom of Israel. David acted with the same sagacity that had characterized the decision-making of his life, announcing his choice and counseling Solomon to eliminate Joab and Abiathar immediately to solidify his ascendancy. I do not mean to imply that this last action was particularly admirable, but it was strategically effective. The point I am making is that, in his agedness, David was the culmination of what he had been becoming across the years.

There is an awesome interconnectedness to the various stages of life. What we are to be in the future we are becoming now, which means that agedness is not as remote and unrelated as we might think when we are twenty or thirty or forty. One of the points that Dr. Segler emphasized in his book is that we not wait until we are sixty-five to begin to get ready for agedness. All of life is a preparation for the final and climactic act, so it is never too soon to begin to get ready for this stage.

So, exactly what is the unique challenge in "the evening" or final stages of life? In his famous essay, "The Eight Ages of Man," Erik Erickson defines this last growth-challenge as achieving "ego-integrity." And just what does he mean by this rather abstract term? I think he is talking about achieving a positive and hopeful perspective about three things—one's own personhood, one's life, and one's death. The concept could also be described as a coming to a sense of peace and satisfaction about one's worth, one's past, and one's future. When you stop and think about it, are not these qualities the mirror opposites of despair? What is that dark state, if not the feeling that one's personhood has no worth, that one's past is a bleak failure, and that the future holds nothing of promise to which to look forward? Coming to the opposite of such conclusions—that is, being able to bless one's self in terms of personhood and past and future—is what "ego-integrity" means. Dag Hammarskjöld said: "For all that has been, thanks! For all that will be, yes!" The person who can join him wholeheartedly in that statement has come to the pinnacle of human maturity, and in the terms of the Psalmist, has so numbered his days that he has gained a heart of wisdom (Psalm 90:12).

Practically speaking, how does one go about achieving such a mature perspective on life? What can we begin doing, here and now, so that we shall be able to feel such positive things about the entirety of our existence?

At this point the Christian gospel can be extraordinarily useful indeed, for it speaks of *grace* and *providence* and *hope*, and these realities are uniquely related to the issues of self and past and future. For example, the answer to the question of personal worth can be found in an understanding of God's grace. This is the secret of true security and self-esteem. Once, in a group of which I was a part, the leader asked each one of us: "What is the most important single thing about you? What are you depending on the most when you die and stand before your Maker? Is it your family name, or your accomplishments, or your possessions or what?" That kind of probing was very revealing to me, for I came to see that anything less than the grace of God would not be sufficient in such a moment.

In the final analysis, it is what God has made of us, not what we have made of ourselves, that is our hope. And the way to prepare for a positive perspective on self at the end is to begin now to ground our lives and hopes in the reality of grace, not in works. Saint Paul said: "By the grace of God, I am what I am." This realization stands us in good stead in the evening of life.

Paul Tournier observed that agedness is that time of life when the focus of living shifts from doing and having to being. Quite often a senior citizen does not have the strength or opportunity to do as he or she once did, nor does the possession of certain things seem that important. After all, if one is bedridden and almost blind, what difference does it make if there is a Jaguar sedan in the driveway or a hundred suits in the closet? As life at this stage focuses down to the reality of being, how satisfying it is to know that one's worth comes ultimately from the love God has for us, rather than from what we do or have or can earn. To have settled early in life that it is by grace we are saved, not by works, is the best preparation I know for the positive self-perspective so essential to the evening of life. The waters of grace will support our whole weight if we can learn to trust them. Happy is the person who does not wait until he is sixty-five to discover the basis of such self-esteem.

The second thing in the gospel that contributes to this kind of perspective is what I call providence, or the belief that life is destiny and not just a process of blind chance. This means coming to believe that in all things God has been at work for good. It is not just the pleasures and triumphs that bear the mark of God's hand, but all events—the bad as well as the good. Real maturity is achieved when the bittersweet quality of all existence is accepted rather than resented. "All sunshine makes a desert," states an old Arab proverb; wise is the person who comes to realize this fact and begins to acknowledge hardship as "the elder brother of good."

A young woman reminiscing about her youthful days once wrote: "I loved my uncle's ranch when I was a child! There was space to run unhampered, freedom to explore. The dust lay inches thick upon the trails, and running barefoot down the path of sifting powder was a sumptuous sort of feeling. The barn was my playground, full of animated toys. In the loft there were hay and mice and fairly friendly spiders. The mint grew wild and plush beside the creek, and my aunt made berry pies and the smell would seek me out wherever I played around the house. I rode my cousin's palomino horse through fantasies that never seems to end. If I am not careful, Lord, I can edit out these memories and forget that I got a bee sting where I picked the mint and burned my tongue time and time again on the berry pies because I never seemed to learn and couldn't wait. Or that the barn smelled just awful or that the horse made my bottom sore and the dust that felt like sifted powder made me sneeze all summer. If I'm not careful, I can forget all these things. But if I'm wise, I will remember that *all of life has both of these things in it."*

It is very important that we never conclude that only the pleasant and the beautiful have positive value. The truth of the matter is that life is a bittersweet reality, and that is its essence and its glory. For the final outcome both the sunshine and the shadows are needed.

A belief in providence, in a God who is at work in all things for good, can lead to that perspective on the past that enables one to say: "For all that has been, thanks!" It is one thing to look back and say: "For *some* of what has been, thanks!" To embrace all of life in that thanksgiving is something quite different, but it is the perspective that a belief in God's goodness and wisdom provides. Understanding life as destiny, not happenstance, and acknowledging God's hand as having been *in it all*, does make for gratitude, acceptance and the ability to end one's days at peace with the past.

One further gospel reality is involved here, and that is the power of hope—the ability to look toward the future and even toward death with positive expectancy. Reuel Howe tells of visiting with an old friend who was nearing death. The man, fully aware of his condition, said quite calmly, "You know, I am amazed at how all this is working out. I had always wondered what it was going to be like to die, but lo and behold, it does not seem all that unusual. Death has turned out to be an old acquaintance in different garb." He went on to say, "For years now, I have undergone experiences that seem similar. From my earliest days, I had to learn to let go of some things that I had in order to get some of the things I did not have. This is what I did the day I started to school or left home to go to work or launched out on a new career. It turns out I have died a thousand deaths across the years, and in all of these experiences I have learned something: *every exit is also an entrance*! You never leave one place without being given another. There is always new life on the other side of the door, and this is my faith as far as death is concerned. I have walked this way before. Death is an exit, to be sure, but at the same time, it is also an entrance."

I cannot think of a finer image of hope than linking "exit" and "entrance" together. The way this man came to such hope is significant as well. As he said, the last challenge of life is not so different from what we face again and again in our pilgrimage. Beginning in earliest childhood, we do have to die to smaller worlds if we are to reach bigger ones; and in every case, there is life on the other side of these crises of risk and growth. No exit ever leads us out to nowhere. Every exit is also an entrance, and learning this fact is what gives a person hope and the ability to say: "For all that will be, yes!"

This is what I think Erik Erikson means by the phrase *ego-integrity* as opposed to despair. The final challenge of our earthly existence is coming to a positive and hopeful perspective about ourselves, our past and our future. How can we do this? The Gospel offers three indispensable resources: grace, providence and hope. It enables us to say three things: First, "By the grace of God, I am what I am." That statement speaks to the issue of self-worth. Secondly, "For all that has been, thanks!" That statement speaks to the past. And finally, "For all that will be, yes!" That statement speaks to the future. This is what "ego-integrity" is all about, and from the account in 1 Chronicles, it appears that David achieved this goal, for we are told: "He died in a good old age, full of days, riches and honor" (29:28).

The truth of the matter is that you and I can do the very same thing. The time to begin to prepare for that kind of ending is right now. It involves learning to ground our whole existence in the grace of God. It involves coming to believe that life is destiny, and that in all things—the bitter and the sweet—God is at work for good. It involves learning through a thousand little deaths and resurrections that every exit is also an entrance.

Isn't it time, then, to learn of grace, to learn of providence, to learn of hope? Right here is the secret, not just of good living, but of good dying as well.

Well, what are we waiting for—?

To schedule Dr. John Claypool for a speaking engagement contact:

McKinney Associates, Inc.
P.O. Box 5162
Louisville, KY 40255-0162

Phone: 1-800-955-0162
Web: www.mckinneyspeakers.com

Insight Press publishes three others books by Dr. John Claypool:

*Glad Reunion: Meeting Ourselves in the Lives of
    Biblical Men and Women*
The Preaching Event
Tracks of a Fellow Struggler

To order or obtain information contact:

Insight Press
P.O. Box 8369
New Orleans, LA 70182

Phone: 985-727-1638
Fax: 985-727-3532